Elephants Can't Jump

and other poems about animals

Compiled by Brian Moses
Illustrated by Neal Layton

Belitha Press

Contents

Elephants Can't Jump

and other poems about animals

For the children and staff at
Robsack Wood C.P. School,
St Leonards-on-Sea

First published in Great Britain in 2001 by

Belitha Press Limited,
London House, Great Eastern Wharf
Parkgate Road, London SW11 4NQ

This collection © Brian Moses 2001
Illustrations © Neal Layton 2001

Series editors: Pie Corbett, Mary-Jane Wilkins
Editors: Stephanie Turnbull, Russell Mclean
Designer: Sarah Goodwin

ISBN 1 84138 246 9 (hardback)
ISBN 1 84138 256 6 (paperback)

British Library Cataloguing in Publication Data
for this book is available from the British Library.

Printed by Omnia Books Ltd, Glasgow

10 9 8 7 6 5 4 3 2 1

Elephants Can't Jump

Elephants can't jump, and that's a fact.
So it's no good expecting an elephant to jump for joy
if you tell him some good news.
You won't make an elephant jump
if you sound a loud noise behind him –
elephants can't jump.
You won't see an elephant skipping or pole-vaulting.
It wasn't an elephant that jumped over the moon
when the little dog laughed,
and contrary to popular belief
elephants do not jump when they see mice.
Elephants, with their great bulk,
don't like to leave the ground.
Elephants and jumping do not go well together.

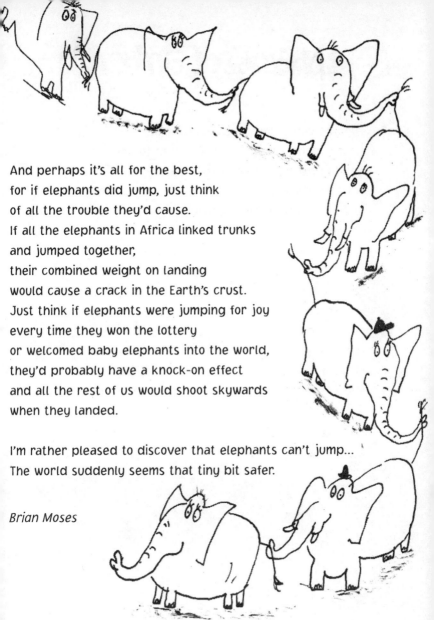

And perhaps it's all for the best,
for if elephants did jump, just think
of all the trouble they'd cause.
If all the elephants in Africa linked trunks
and jumped together,
their combined weight on landing
would cause a crack in the Earth's crust.
Just think if elephants were jumping for joy
every time they won the lottery
or welcomed baby elephants into the world,
they'd probably have a knock-on effect
and all the rest of us would shoot skywards
when they landed.

I'm rather pleased to discover that elephants can't jump...
The world suddenly seems that tiny bit safer.

Brian Moses

Elephants can't jump.

One Eye Open...

And lo, god made the ocean,
And lo, god made the sea,
And lo, god said, 'Dear dolphin,
Keep an eye on it for me?'

Judy Tweddle

Dolphins always keep one eye open when they sleep.

Imagine...

being a swift,

scything the air,
swooping, zooming,
catching your breakfast
as you go.

Imagine yourself

asleep on the wing,
nodding off in Basingstoke
or Oxford,
and hours later
waking up twittering

(what if you hadn't meant
to go there!)

in Wigan,
Newcastle
or even John o'Groats.

Matt Simpson

Swifts can sleep while they are flying.

The Seven Brains of the Caterpillar

My first brain thinks the colour of my skin;
Dresses me as green as lettuce.
My second brain arranges crawling;
One slow sucker foot. Hump and wriggle.
Brain three says eat.
Four lullabies me.
Five dreams my breathing;
Lets the wet air suck sweetly in and out.
Six senses danger;
Rolls me up bud-tight at a touch.
But seven lies still. Does nothing. Bides.
It will spin me a shroud, set me my coffin.
Pupa. Pupa. Sound it like a pulse.
From this dead shell I will be born again.
A butterfly. An angel.

Jan Dean

Simple animals – such as caterpillars – don't have one big brain.
They have several mini-brains.

The Galapagos Flyers

Give us a sideways look
and use your brain.
You'll realize,
perhaps with quite a shock,
that we were meant to fly.

It's obvious.
Our patterned tortoise shells
are curved on top,
designed to streamline quickly flowing air,
and underneath we're flat as boards,
just like the wings of planes
when looked at from the side.

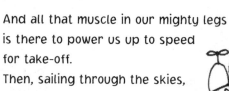

And all that muscle in our mighty legs
is there to power us up to speed
for take-off.
Then, sailing through the skies,
we'd pull our droop-snoot heads
and trailing feet inside our shells
and, sunshine-flashing UFOs,
we'd ride and rise
in currents of warm air.

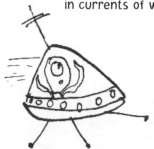

We were meant to fly,
but when they shared the land out
here on Earth
they lost the plot
and dumped us on these island lumps of rock
with no room anywhere
for runways
and nowhere near to fly to,
as far as we can see.

We were never meant to swim:
in early days,
fed up with pterodactyls acting cool,
some of our wannabe sky-surfers
frisbeed themselves from a high cliff,
fell in the sea,
turned turtle
and landed in the soup.

But we WERE meant to fly.

Brian Davies

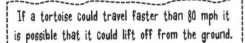

If a tortoise could travel faster than 80 mph it
is possible that it could lift off from the ground.

African Allsorts

A pack of ELENOCEROS
Racing just in front of us,
A herd of stripy ZEBALO
Trotting very slow,
The roar of the TIGON
A great rock to sit on,
The heavy stamp and pant
Of the massive RHINOPHANT,
And in the lake watching us
Floats a dangerous CROCOPOTAMUS
    Beware beware
    Of the eyes that stare
    And the curious honk
    Of the GIRADONK

Take care to look and look again
At the curious sights on the African plain

Les Baynton

Farmers in Malta have crossed sheep and goats to breed the shoat.

Artistic Giant

It wasn't my idea to take up painting
and I have to admit that when the buckets of paint first appeared
I thought they were Smartie flavoured milk-shakes
and tasted them. Talk about red faced!
(Actually it was more yellow, blue *and* red faced!)

My first attempts at dabbling in oils
were portraits of my friend Dumbo
but very soon I was trying my trunk at landscapes and
various still life arrangements of fruits and flowers.

I thought my early efforts were pretty good for a beginner
until I overheard one of our art assistants talking to a visitor –
he called my paintings abstracts!
I hadn't realized they were *that* good!
And the visitor, who immediately took out his wallet
to buy one of my larger works,
called me an artistic giant.

Well – what a boost to my creative confidence!
But I haven't let my new found fame as a great artist go to my head.
The beret?
What beret?
Oh that – that's just a little thing to help keep the sun off my head.

Philip Waddell

Paintings by elephants at a sanctuary in Chiang Mai,
Thailand, are sold to pay for the elephants' upkeep.

No Lips

Crocodiles have no lips
So they can't kiss.
No puckering up
No pursed pecking
No slurpy smackaroonies
No squelchy sink plunger suckering
But then again...
Who'd want to snog a croc?

Paul Cookson

Crocodiles have no lips, so their fearsome
teeth are visible at all times.

The Kid's Lot

Poor little wide-awake,
Missing those bedtime stories,
Can't close its eyes,
And visit never-never land.
It's all mountaineering,
And hanging from the edge of a ledge.
That's the kid's lot.
Onwards and upwards,
Expected to achieve the highest goal,
Plant your goat's beard on the hilltop.
And how the kid must envy the kitten,
Whose eyes are shut when open,
Whose life is one long nap.
Poor insomniac,
Poor mite,
No wonder its hair has turned white.

Mary Green

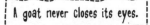

A goat never closes its eyes.

49

A Llama Alarmer

A llama, a llama
will keep your sheep calmer –
yes that's what a llama will do.
It's not just a charmer
it can be an alarmer
and see off a hungry bear too.

There's no need of armour
if you keep a llama.
It's not just a big snooty sheep.
So go get your pyjamas
you weary old farmers.
At last you can stop counting sheep.

Yes a llama, a llama's
a friend to the farmer,
a friend to the chicken and sheep.
No panic and drama
if you have a llama –
just sweet dreams, quiet fields... and deep sleep.

Michaela Morgan

One way of stopping predators from eating farm animals is to keep a llama to protect them. Llamas chase predators away and try to stamp on them.

The Flight of the Bumble Bee

The bumble bee with tiny wings,
so heavy from her nose to sting,
it's been proved, it's science fact,
she cannot fly – and that is that.

So when you see her buzzing by,
weighed down with pollen on her thigh,
held up by whizzing unseen wings –
she's not flying – you're seeing things!

Liz Brownlee

According to the theory of aerodynamics, the size, shape and weight
of a bumble bee in relation to its wingspan make flying impossible.

Archer Fish

They would not care to live in the open sea.
It's the mangrove swamps for them,
The archers.
Outlaws.
Target practice every day
With water pistols at the ready –
Take aim.
Fire!
Bullseye!
The young ones often miss, of course,
But they will learn.
Nobody tells them off for spitting.

Sue Cowling

The archer fish catches insects by spitting out a jet
of water to knock its prey from overhanging branches.

Invitation

Dear Buffalo,

You are invited ~~for~~ **to** my birthday lunch next ~~Munchday~~ **Monday**.

Your presence ~~on~~ **at** my table would be my greatest ~~dish~~ **wish**.

You will be served a delicious ~~buffalo~~ **buffet** meal,

followed by instant ~~death~~ **dessert**.

You are welcome to stay overnight in my ~~stomach~~ **studio flat**, which

can always stretch to accommodate my biggest ~~meals~~ **mates**.

Looking forward to ~~eating~~ **meeting** you, and hoping to find you in top form!

Yours ~~never~~

Python

Kate Williams

A python can eat a whole buffalo without chewing it.

Sing Hi for the Ugly Jawless Fishes

Sing hi for the ugly jawless fishes   *sea lamprey*
   That would look so revolting if served on dishes.
Sing ho for the croc with a frying pan head   *gharial*
   And the snoozy sea otter tied up in bed.

Sing hi for the snake that drowns its prey,   *anaconda*
   And the smelliest beastie that stinks all day. *zorilla*
Sing ho for the ostrich's elastic throat
   That's been known to swallow an overcoat!

Sing hi for the long-necks that climb the high skies, *whooper swans*
    Or the frightened lizards squirting blood from their eyes. *horned toads*
Sing hi for the foraging fox in the town,
    And for the roosting bird that sleeps upside down. *blue-crowned hanging parrot*

Sing hi for the bird that flies in all weathers, *albatross*
    Or the weird water bird that eats its own feathers. *western grebe*
Sing ho for the sleepy fish snoozing on the rock, *triggerfish*
    And for the electric eel's habit of giving a shock!

Sing hi for the cockroach that will even eat toenails,
    Or the long spiralled tusk of the fencing narwhals.
Sing ho for the monkey with the longest nose *proboscis monkey*
    And the improbable mammal with forty-five toes! *forty-five toed mammal (no such thing, but all the other facts are true)*

John Rice

28

Incredible Sole

And now! Please
Ladies and Gentlemen,
It is my pleasure to introduce to you,
All the way from the ocean floor,
That disguiser from the depths,
That chameleon of the coral,
The Incredible Sole!

For his first trick
The Incredible Sole
Lies on his flat and floppy tummy
On this black-and-white checkered
chess board.
We count slowly to 100
And, remarkably,
Without mirrors, without tricks,
The black-and-white pattern
Appears on his back!

Thank you! Thank you!

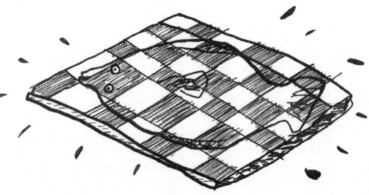

And now,
For his second trick,
The Incredible Sole
Lies on his flat and floppy tummy
On this multicoloured Monopoly board.
We count slowly to 100
And, remarkably,
Without mirrors, without tricks,
On his back, you can clearly read:
'King's Cross Station £200'.

Thank you! You're very kind!

And for his final trick
The Incredible Sole
Lies on his flat and floppy tummy
On this prettily patterned plate,
Which I place in the oven
At 180°C; Gas Mark 4.
We count slowly to 100
And my dinner is cooked and ready!
Ho! Ho! Ho!
It works every time.

now, who's going to get the chips?

Paul Bright

If a sole lies on a chess board, it can change the colouring of its body
to match the pattern on the chess board in about four minutes.

The Axolotl

You are the Peter Pan
of the silent world
Where secret rivers flow
Through hidden caves,
And sinister rocks stare
With hollow eyes.

You flutter the pale wings
Of your gills
And gaze at your own
Never Land,
While bats rise like lost children
And stalactites loom
Like the sails of tall ships.

Brave Axolotl
With your eyes full of dreams,
I wish I could be like you
And never grow up,
Never grow up.

Clare Bevan

An axolotl is a salamander that never becomes an adult.

Amorous Octopus

The
octopus
with eight
arms pleases
lovers with his
hugs and squeezes.
He needs so many
cuddling parts because
he has three
loving hearts.

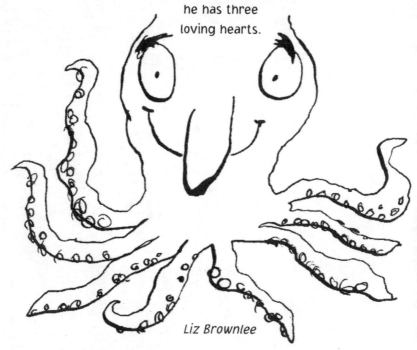

Liz Brownlee

An octopus has two 'gill hearts' which pump blood through its single gill (similar to our lungs) and into its main heart.

Don't Judge a Bird by Her Looks

The most beautiful eggs in the world
– they are violet and greenish and blue –
are laid by a dull lumpy bird
by the name of the Great Tinamou.

She is not a good bird in the air,
she is clumsy and weak, but she copes.
And she serves as a brilliant reminder
of what you can do with high hopes.

Judy Tweddle

The Great Tinamou lives in the rainforests of Mexico, Bolivia and Brazil. It lays beautifully-coloured eggs.

Dragonfly

Left, no right – down,
now back up... here, over here, no there –
against the dark trees –
a bolt of blue, electric shock blue,
soars, drops, dashes about,
hold on! He's up there!

Wings whirring like... wait...
hang on... propellers, yes propellers.
They show up like grey mist
around this blue stick. Steals out, unseen,
out over the sunny pond.
Skims, and then U-turns, doubles back.

Just a sec... his soundtrack's a choral hum,
this flying hologram
who's never still for...
overhead, now beyond, phew!

He's been around... whoosh...
whistles past, since before the dinosaurs
who lorded about in wind tunnel canyons:
he tempted their claws and paws
with his dive-bombing and fly-pasts,
spurting away, putting his foot down,
Mach-2 on the animal speedo.

Down to our left,
loses our gaze but suddenly,
within point something of a second,
clips the eye's corner sight
and we lock on to this
inch-long needle of laser blue –
wherever he darts – indecisively –
hovers, nope, moves on,
doesn't settle to anything.

On and on, doesn't stop,
like a speeded-up film of London traffic.
Where does he get all that energy?
Doesn't he have a home to go to?

Dragon – flitting through the centuries,
bobbing about on the back of time – fly!

John Rice

There have been dragonflies for over 200 million years, since before
the dinosaurs. These insects have six legs, but they cannot walk.

The Miracle Walker

It's the lizard that walks on water
the miracle walker, it's true!
The amazing basilisk
light and strong
that lifts itself
on its two hind legs
and madly thrashes along.

Over the water in short, sharp leaps
– what a stupendous sight!
But fast-fast-fast
is the name of the game
if it wants to get it right.
Fast as its gangling toes can go
fast as the eye can blink
for once its speedometer
starts to fall
it slowly
slowly
sinks.

Patricia Leighton

The basilisk can walk on both water and land. It moves so quickly that its long toes get a split-second 'grip' on the surface of the water. As soon as it slows down, it sinks and has to swim.

And the Prize for the Smelliest Creature Goes to...

Imagine that you have not had a bath for a month
Now imagine that you and all your friends have not had
  a bath for a month
Now imagine that you and all your friends who have not
  had a bath for a month
have been left in a small, warm room with no windows on
  a summer's afternoon.
Now imagine that in that small, warm room with no windows
  on a summer's afternoon
are not only you and your unwashed friends
But a sack of mouldy cabbages
and another sack of mouldy cabbages
and another sack of mouldy cabbages
and another sack which does not contain mouldy cabbage
It contains – very, very, very, very ripe Gorgonzola cheese
Then one of your friends, who has not had a bath for a
  month, says,
'Look, I've found a trapdoor – we can escape.'
And so you heave back the trap door
To find it leads straight to a sewer
Which happens to be blocked.
Got the picture?

Well that would be like a garden of flowers
Compared with the pong of
A Rock Hopper Penguin colony.
These birds have a personal hygiene problem
Way beyond the powers of the toughest deodorant.
You can smell them several miles away
So be grateful that they live
On Nightingale Island,
Thousands of miles from here.

John Coldwell

The smell of the Rock Hopper Penguin colony on Nightingale
Island (near Tristan da Cunha) can be detected several miles
downwind and is a useful navigational aid for shipping.

Termites

If you add up all the people
And you add up all their weights,
They only weigh a fraction
Of an insect and his mates
And his mates
And his mates
And his mates
And his mates
And his mates
And his mates
And his mates
And his mates
And his mates
And his mates
And his mates   And his mates
And his mates And his mates
And his mates   And his mates
And his mates And his mates And his mates
And his mates And his mates And his mates And his mates
And his mates   And his mates   And his mates   And his mates

Paul Bright

The world's termite population is ten times heavier than the human population.

Flea Smitten

If I were a flea
Heaven knows what I'd see.
Just one flick does the trick –
Won't catch me!

I could leap over trees;
Flee from feared enemies.
Just two springs! Look no wings!
No grazed knees!

I'd be no humble-bee;
Say 'Goodbye gravity!'
Come up trumps with high jumps –
Fancy-free!

A top-flea pedigree;
Not a dogsbody me.
Up-beat style, armed missile –
Super flea!

Mina Johnson

A flea can jump 130 times its own height.

Four Second Memory

Is it a fact or is it a hype
that a goldfish suffers a memory wipe
every time four seconds passes by
and if it's true, does he wonder why?
Perhaps that's why he's happy to swim
round and round in his tank, nothing bothers him.
Four seconds and then his mind is wiped clean,
four seconds and he's no idea where he's been.
So every circuit's a different view,
every circuit brings something new.
Does he ever get feelings of 'deja-vu'
or say to another fish, 'Don't I know you,
haven't we met some place before?'
But after the four seconds the slam of a door
erases the thought from his memory bank
and he'll take another tour of his tank.

In a goldfish world there could never be
any sense of goldfish history.
They could never follow serials on TV,
their lives must be one big mystery –
What did I do, what have I seen,
who did I meet, where have I been?
Do they suffer four seconds of stress,
could one ever be called as a witness?
'Where were you on the night of the crime?'
He'd really have no notion of time.
Adrift in the water, he's floating and flowing
with only four seconds to know where he's going,
four seconds and then his mind is wiped clean
and the goldfish has no idea where he's been.

Brian Moses

Studies show that goldfish have memories of approximately four seconds.

Salmon Says...

How little you use your senses,
Though you think yourselves so advanced!
Have you savoured the waves of the ocean
For the flavour of your first dance?
Have you traced the taste through reeking deeps
To the waters where you were born?
We have swum thousands of briny miles
To leap upstream to spawn.

When salmon are ready to lay their eggs, they swim thousands
of miles to return to the spot in the river where they were born.

And now we are proud of our offspring,
They will dance their parents' dance.
They, too, will follow the scent back home.
We salmon leave nothing to chance.
Poor you, with your cars and ships and planes;
Your rockets that fly to the moon!
You can't even smell or taste your way
To yesterday afternoon!

Celia Warren

Streetwise Skunk

I'm a streetwise skunk,
don't take no lip,
from the trucks and lorries
at the Council tip.

See them rumbling
down the yard,
crunching their gears,
trying to look hard.

Dust and noise
in the danger zone,
but I'm not leaving my
'Home Sweet Home'.

Here I stand
and here I stay.
I lift my tail
and use my spray.

A secret weapon
with a dreadful smell.
What's it like?
It's hard to tell...

Think of greens
and brussel sprouts,
cooked in a room
with the lights turned out.

Stink bomb clouds
and garlic streams.
Monster smells
that haunt your dreams.

Flaky Zombies
with sweaty socks.
That's my *Special*,
it really rocks!

Big hairy dustmen
take one sniff,
then long to leap
from the nearest cliff.

They look shaky,
hold their noses,
talk through mouths
like garden hoses.

49

It's a Wild West movie,
action all day,
in every showdown,
I'm quick on the spray!

I stand strong,
it's really no sweat,
'til the last truck runs
into the sunset.

At the end of the day,
I've always won.
Made a lot of fuss,
had a lot of fun.
Yes indeed,
I'm number one!

I'm a streetwise skunk,
don't take no lip.
I'm the king
of the Council tip!

I said...

I'm the king
of the Council tip!!

Note:
This poem was written in *Smellyrhymearoma*.
To enjoy the full 'skunky' atmosphere, just sniff your
feet as you read it...!

Tony Norman

Skunks are stubborn. When faced with danger, they stand
their ground... and use their foul-smelling spray!

Dreamless

The snake can't look forward to his dreams coming true,
Can't sing to his darling, 'sweet dreams of you',
Can't dream of a Christmas, white or otherwise,
And when he is sleeping, cannot fantasize,
Can't travel in dreamland to far away shores,
In his sleep cannot open imagination's closed doors,
No scenes beyond waking unfold in his mind,
And when he is sleeping, the snake you will find
Will not have a nightmare, won't wake with a scream,
For a snake is a reptile, and reptiles can't dream.

Valerie Bloom

Snakes can't dream.

A Hippo Got There First

'Taxi!' cried the tourist,
then stood and stamped and cursed,
for as she ran to get inside,
a hippo got there first.

'Ice creams,' yelled the ice cream man.
Kids very nearly burst
running to be first in line
but a hippo got there first.

Men raced to reach the winning post
but now they're being nursed
in bandages with muscle strain
for a hippo got there first.

Athletes ran cross country
with great distances traversed
but they ended up disgruntled
when a hippo got there first.

A hunter stalked a hippo.
Its reaction was adverse.
The hunter ran, but sadly,
the hippo got there first.

They don't possess an athlete's shape.
Their figures are the worst
but if you race a hippo,
the hippo will be first.

Marian Swinger

A hippo can run at 20 mph – faster than most humans.

How Alpacas Make Their Point

When they're feeling obstinate
Or if they're in a grump
Alpacas sag and bend their knees
And down they sit – *ker-whump.*

Though you try to change their minds
With pleas or gentle nudging,
Once they're seated on the ground
Alpacas don't like budging.

If you take one for a walk
Prepare to spend all day.
'I think I'll just alpack this in,'
Alpaca says, half-way.

You could try it. Sit down hard
When someone hassles you.
Do it with *alpackitude* –
That's what alpacas do.

Linda Newbery

When alpacas don't want to do something,
they fold their legs and sit down on the ground.

Amazing Lies

An ape can smell a sausage
   from a thousand miles away.
It likes it green as spinach
   in a sick state of decay.

There's a fish in a southern ocean
   (so it's often said)
that dines on toasted Mother's Pride
   and five other kinds of bread

while rats and mice and hamsters
   (believe this if you like)
brmm brmm brmm like maniacs
   on a Harley Davidson bike.

A young Manx cat can survive a jump
   from the top of the Post Office Tower.
Skunks get fresh as a scarlet rose
   by taking a champagne shower.

A tortoise will give a talk tonight
    at the House of Commons, and
an eagle will often escape from a crab
    by digging its beak in the sand.

When you look close at a porcupine
    remember this, if you will:
there's a letter from Father Christmas hidden
    in every elegant quill.

My dog sings when it's chasing cats.
   A bee mimes as it flies.
The rest of the facts in this book are true –

   I thought it needed some lies.

Fred Sedgwick

Index of titles and first lines

First lines are in italics

Index of authors

Acknowledgements

Les Baynton: 'African Allsorts' © Les Baynton. **Clare Bevan**: 'The Axolotl' © Clare Bevan. **Valerie Bloom**: 'Dreamless' © Valerie Bloom. **Paul Bright**: 'Incredible Sole' and 'Termites' © Paul Bright. **Liz Brownlee**: 'Amorous Octopus' and 'The Flight of the Bumble Bee' © Liz Brownlee. **John Coldwell**: 'And the Prize for the Smelliest Creature Goes to...' © John Coldwell. **Paul Cookson**: 'No Lips' © Paul Cookson. **Sue Cowling**: 'Archer Fish' © Sue Cowling. **Brian Davies**: 'The Galapagos Flyers' © Brian Davies. **Jan Dean**: 'The Seven Brains of the Caterpillar' © Jan Dean. **Mary Green**: 'The Kid's Lot' © Mary Green. **Mina Johnson**: 'Flea Smitten' © Mina Johnson. **Patricia Leighton**: 'The Miracle Walker' © Patricia Leighton. **Michaela Morgan**: 'A Llama Alarmer' © Michaela Morgan. **Brian Moses**: 'Elephants Can't Jump', first published in *Don't Look at Me in That Tone of Voice* (Macmillan), and 'Four Second Memory', first published in *Barking Back at Dogs* (Macmillan), both © Brian Moses. **Linda Newbury**: 'How Alpacas Make Their Point' © Linda Newbury 2001. **Tony Norman**: 'Streetwise Skunk' © Tony Norman. **John Rice**: 'Dragonfly' and 'Sing Hi for the Ugly Jawless Fishes' © John Rice. **Fred Sedgwick**: 'Amazing Lies' © Fred Sedgwick. **Matt Simpson**: 'Imagine...' © Matt Simpson. **Marian Swinger**: 'A Hippo Got There First' © Marian Swinger. **Judy Tweddle**: 'Don't Judge a Bird by Her Looks' and 'One Eye Open...' © Judy Tweddle. **Philip Waddell**: 'Artistic Giant' © Philip Waddell. **Celia Warren**: 'Salmon Says...' © Celia Warren 2001. **Kate Williams**: 'Invitation' © Kate Williams.